Keto Blender Cookbook for Beginners

600 Amazing Recipes for Super-Easy, Super-Healthy Desserts, Soups, Sauces, Drinks and More

Wurly Dather

© Copyright 2021 Wurly Dather - All Rights Reserved.

In no way is it legal to reproduce, duplicate, or transmit any part of this document by either electronic means or in printed format. Recording of this publication is strictly prohibited, and any storage of this material is not allowed unless with written permission from the publisher. All rights reserved.

The information provided herein is stated to be truthful and consistent, in that any liability, regarding inattention or otherwise, by any usage or abuse of any policies, processes, or directions contained within is the solitary and complete responsibility of the recipient reader. Under no circumstances will any legal liability or blame be held against the publisher for any reparation, damages, or monetary loss due to the information herein, either directly or indirectly.

Respective authors own all copyrights not held by the publisher.

Legal Notice:

This book is copyright protected. This is only for personal use. You cannot amend, distribute, sell, use, quote or paraphrase any part of the content within this book without the consent of the author or copyright owner. Legal action will be pursued if this is breached.

Disclaimer Notice:

Please note the information contained within this document is for educational and entertainment purposes only. Every attempt has been made to provide accurate, up-to-date and reliable, complete information. No warranties of any kind are expressed or implied. Readers acknowledge that the author is not engaging in the rendering of legal, financial, medical or professional advice.

By reading this document, the reader agrees that under no circumstances are we responsible for any losses, direct or indirect, which are incurred as a result of the use of information contained within this document, including, but not limited to, errors, omissions, or inaccuracies.

Table of Contents

Chapter 1: Appetizers 6
- Easy Jalapeno Ranch Dip 6
- Curried Cashew Dip 7
- Cannellini Bean Dip 8
- Roasted Pepper Dip 9
- Easy Olive Tapenade 10
- Quick & Easy Black Bean Dip 11
- Cauliflower Artichoke Dip 12
- Creamy Feta Dip 13
- Tomato Chickpeas Hummus 14
- Flavorful Salsa Dip 15
- Healthy Beetroot Dip 16
- Cashew Queso Dip 17
- Perfect Artichoke Dip 18
- Quick Olive Dip 19
- Roasted Pepper Hummus 20
- Spicy Chipotle Ranch Dip 21
- Easy Avocado Dip 22
- Creamy Avocado Dip 23
- Feta Red Pepper Dip 24
- Flavorful Cranberry Salsa 25

Chapter 2: Soups & Salsas 26
- Spicy Squash Soup 26
- Potato Leek Soup 27
- Creamy Asparagus Soup 28
- Delicious Cranberry Salsa 29
- Creamy Squash Soup 30
- Tasty Garden Salsa 31
- Strawberry Salsa 32
- Spicy Chipotle Salsa 33
- Tomatillo Pineapple Salsa 34
- Mango Salsa 35
- Berry Salsa 36
- Cauliflower Soup 37

Chapter 3: Dressing, Sauces & Spreads .. 38
- Enchilada Sauce 38
- Low-carb BBQ Sauce 39
- Mango Lemon Dressing 40
- Chickpea Pepper Spread 41
- Flavorful Peanut Sauce 42
- Creamy Avocado Dressing 43
- Avocado Sandwich Spread 44
- Classic Caesar Dressing 45
- Creamy Tomatillo Dressing 46
- Southwest Dressing 47
- Mango Mustard Sauce 48
- Chimichurri Sauce 49
- Creamy Avocado Sauce 50
- Honey Mustard Dressing 51
- Zesty Chipotle Ranch Dressing 52

Cheese Pepper Spread 53
Vegan Greek Dressing 54
Easy Hollandaise Sauce 55

Chapter 4: Desserts 56
Mango Sorbet 56
Blueberry Ice Cream 57
Strawberry Banana Sorbet 58
Perfect Pineapple Ice Cream 59
Easy Strawberry Ice Cream 60
Pumpkin Mousse 61
Fluffy Strawberry Mousse 62
Chocolate Mousse 63
Orange Pineapple Sorbet 64
Yummy Blueberry Yogurt 65
Strawberry Cheesecake Ice Cream 66
Pineapple Mango Sorbet 67
Coconut Popsicles 68
Easy Lemon Curd 69
Coconut Cherry Popsicles 70
Easy Cherry Sorbet 71
Easy Pumpkin Mousse 72
Peach Ice Cream 73
Nutella Banana Ice Cream 74
Raspberry Sorbet 75
Raspberry Mousse 76
Blueberry Sorbet 77

Chapter 5: Drinks 78
Banana Coffee Smoothie 78
Peach Raspberry Smoothie 79
Coffee Milkshake 80
Watermelon Strawberry Smoothie 81
Mix Berry Smoothie 82
Healthy Tropical Smoothie 83
Healthy Berry Smoothie 84
Easy Strawberry Protein Shake 85
Healthy Orange Smoothie 86
Peach Lemonade 87
Mango Pineapple Peach Smoothie ... 88
Cinnamon Apple Smoothie 89
Banana Peanut Butter Smoothie 90
Healthy Avocado Spinach Smoothie .. 91
Sweet Avocado Smoothie 92
Healthy Raspberry Smoothie 93
Spinach Cucumber Smoothie 94
Healthy Oatmeal Smoothie 95
Mango Strawberry Smoothie 96
Cookie Shake 97
Watermelon Strawberry Smoothie ... 98
Cinnamon Banana Smoothie 99
Thick & Creamy Banana Smoothie 100
Creamy Cherry Smoothie 101
Green Pineapple Smoothie 102

Creamy Strawberry Milkshake 103

Banana Kiwi Smoothie 104

Easy Pineapple Lemonade 105

Chapter 1: Appetizers

Easy Jalapeno Ranch Dip

Preparation Time: 5 minutes
Cooking Time: 1 minute
Serve: 4

Ingredients:

- 8 oz can jalapeno peppers with juice
- 1 cup sour cream
- 1 cup mayonnaise
- 1/2 tsp garlic powder
- 1/4 cup fresh cilantro
- 1/2 tsp pepper
- 1 tsp salt

Directions:

1. Add all ingredients into the blender container. Secure the lid.
2. Start the blending at low speed, then quickly increase to highest speed and blend until smooth.
3. Serve and enjoy.

Nutritional Value (Amount per Serving):

- Calories 354
- Fat 31.7 g
- Carbohydrates 17 g
- Sugar 4 g
- Protein 2.5 g
- Cholesterol 41 mg

Curried Cashew Dip

Preparation Time: 5 minutes
Cooking Time: 1 minute
Serve: 8

Ingredients:

- 1 cup cashews
- 1/8 tsp white pepper
- 1/8 tsp garlic powder
- 1/8 tsp cayenne
- 1/2 tsp curry powder
- 1 lemon zest
- 3 tbsp fresh lemon juice
- 1/3 cup full-fat coconut milk
- 3/4 cup mayonnaise
- Salt

Directions:

1. Add all ingredients into the blender container. Secure the lid.
2. Start the blending at low speed, then quickly increase to highest speed and blend until smooth.
3. Serve and enjoy.

Nutritional Value (Amount per Serving):

- Calories 257
- Fat 22.6 g
- Carbohydrates 13.5 g
- Sugar 3.6 g
- Protein 3.7 g
- Cholesterol 6 mg

Cannellini Bean Dip

Preparation Time: 5 minutes
Cooking Time: 1 minute
Serve: 8

Ingredients:

- 1 cup can cannellini beans, drained
- 4 tbsp tahini
- 1 lemon juice
- 1 1/2 tsp ground cumin
- 1/4 cup olive oil
- 1/4 cup water
- 2 garlic cloves
- 1 cup can chickpeas, drained
- Salt

Directions:

1. Add all ingredients into the blender container. Secure the lid.
2. Start the blending at low speed, then quickly increase to highest speed and blend until smooth.
3. Serve and enjoy.

Nutritional Value (Amount per Serving):

- Calories 168
- Fat 10.8 g
- Carbohydrates 14.2 g
- Sugar 0.4 g
- Protein 4.9 g
- Cholesterol 0 mg

Roasted Pepper Dip

Preparation Time: 5 minutes
Cooking Time: 1 minute
Serve: 12

Ingredients:

- 16 oz roasted red bell peppers, drained
- 1/4 tsp red pepper flakes
- 1 tsp paprika
- 1 tbsp honey
- 1 tbsp lime juice
- 1 tbsp extra-virgin olive oil
- 2 garlic cloves
- 1 1/2 cups walnuts, roasted
- Salt

Directions:

1. Add all ingredients into the blender container. Secure the lid.
2. Start the blending at low speed, then quickly increase to highest speed and blend until smooth.
3. Serve and enjoy.

Nutritional Value (Amount per Serving):

- Calories 138
- Fat 12.2 g
- Carbohydrates 7.1 g
- Sugar 2.9 g
- Protein 5 g
- Cholesterol 0 mg

Easy Olive Tapenade

Preparation Time: 5 minutes
Cooking Time: 1 minute
Serve: 4

Ingredients:

- 2 cups olives, pitted
- 1/4 cup olive oil
- 1 tbsp fresh lemon juice
- 2 tbsp parsley
- 1 tbsp fresh basil
- 2 garlic cloves
- 1 tbsp capers
- 1/4 cup sun-dried tomatoes, drained

Directions:

1. Add all ingredients into the blender container. Secure the lid.
2. Start the blending at low speed, then quickly increase to highest speed and blend for 1 minute or until getting the desired consistency.
3. Serve and enjoy.

Nutritional Value (Amount per Serving):

- Calories 192
- Fat 19.9 g
- Carbohydrates 5.5 g
- Sugar 0.4 g
- Protein 0.9 g
- Cholesterol 0 mg

Quick & Easy Black Bean Dip

Preparation Time: 5 minutes
Cooking Time: 1 minute
Serve: 8

Ingredients:

- 30 oz can black beans, drained
- 1/4 tsp onion powder
- 1/4 tsp smoked paprika
- 1/4 tsp ground cumin
- 1/2 tsp chili powder
- 1 1/2 tsp garlic, minced
- 1 tbsp fresh lime juice
- 1/2 cup fire-roasted tomatoes, diced
- 1/2 tsp salt

Directions:

1. Add all ingredients into the blender container. Secure the lid.
2. Start the blending at low speed, then quickly increase to highest speed and blend for 1 minute or until getting the desired consistency.
3. Serve and enjoy.

Nutritional Value (Amount per Serving):

- Calories 105
- Fat 0.8 g
- Carbohydrates 19.7 g
- Sugar 1.2 g
- Protein 5.8 g
- Cholesterol 0 mg

Cauliflower Artichoke Dip

Preparation Time: 5 minutes
Cooking Time: 1 minute
Serve: 8

Ingredients:

- 2 cups artichoke hearts
- 1/2 cup cauliflower florets, cooked
- 3 cups spinach, chopped
- 2 tsp nutritional yeast
- 1/3 cup vegetable broth
- 1/2 cup coconut cream, softened
- 3 garlic cloves, minced
- 1 onion, diced
- 2 tbsp olive oil
- 1 tsp salt

Directions:

1. Add all ingredients into the blender container. Secure the lid.
2. Start the blending at low speed, then quickly increase to highest speed and blend for 1 minute or until getting the desired consistency.
3. Serve and enjoy.

Nutritional Value (Amount per Serving):

- Calories 95
- Fat 7.3 g
- Carbohydrates 7 g
- Sugar 1.6 g
- Protein 2.6 g
- Cholesterol 0 mg

Creamy Feta Dip

Preparation Time: 5 minutes
Cooking Time: 1 minute
Serve: 4

Ingredients:

- 7 oz feta cheese, drained
- 1/2 tsp lemon zest
- 1 tbsp olive oil
- 1/2 cup sour cream
- Pepper
- Salt

Directions:

1. Add all ingredients into the blender container. Secure the lid.
2. Start the blending at low speed, then quickly increase to highest speed and blend until smooth & creamy.
3. Serve and enjoy.

Nutritional Value (Amount per Serving):

- Calories 223
- Fat 20.1 g
- Carbohydrates 3.3 g
- Sugar 2.1 g
- Protein 8 g
- Cholesterol 57 mg

Tomato Chickpeas Hummus

Preparation Time: 5 minutes
Cooking Time: 1 minute
Serve: 8

Ingredients:

- 14 oz can chickpeas, drained & rinsed
- 1/2 tsp onion powder
- 1/2 tsp dried basil
- 1/2 tsp dried oregano
- 2 tbsp fresh lime juice
- 2 garlic cloves
- 1/4 cup tahini
- 1/3 cup aquafaba
- 1/3 cup sun-dried tomatoes
- Pepper
- Salt

Directions:

1. Add all ingredients into the blender container. Secure the lid.
2. Start the blending at low speed, then quickly increase to highest speed and blend until smooth.
3. Serve and enjoy.

Nutritional Value (Amount per Serving):

- Calories 110
- Fat 4.6 g
- Carbohydrates 14.5 g
- Sugar 0.5 g
- Protein 3.9 g
- Cholesterol 0 mg

Flavorful Salsa Dip

Preparation Time: 5 minutes
Cooking Time: 1 minute
Serve: 10

Ingredients:

- 1 cup salsa
- 1 cup fresh cilantro
- 2 tsp taco seasoning
- 3/4 cup sour cream

Directions:

1. Add all ingredients into the blender container. Secure the lid.
2. Start the blending at low speed, then quickly increase to highest speed and blend until smooth.
3. Serve and enjoy.

Nutritional Value (Amount per Serving):

- Calories 119
- Fat 7.8 g
- Carbohydrates 7.8 g
- Sugar 0.8 g
- Protein 5.1 g
- Cholesterol 19 mg

Healthy Beetroot Dip

Preparation Time: 5 minutes
Cooking Time: 1 minute
Serve: 8

Ingredients:

- 1 cup pickled beets, drain the liquid
- 20 oz can white beans, drained
- 1 1/2 tbsp vinegar
- 1/4 cup olive oil
- 2 garlic cloves
- 3 tbsp fresh lemon juice
- 1 tbsp lemon zest
- 1/3 cup tahini
- 1/2 tsp salt

Directions:

1. Add all ingredients into the blender container. Secure the lid.
2. Start the blending at low speed, then quickly increase to highest speed and blend until smooth.
3. Serve and enjoy.

Nutritional Value (Amount per Serving):

- Calories 207
- Fat 11.9 g
- Carbohydrates 22.4 g
- Sugar 4.4 g
- Protein 7.2 g
- Cholesterol 0 mg

Cashew Queso Dip

Preparation Time: 5 minutes
Cooking Time: 1 minute
Serve: 8

Ingredients:

- 1 cup cashews
- 1/2 tsp chili powder
- 1 garlic clove
- 1/2 tsp paprika
- 1 tsp onion powder
- 1/3 cup marinara sauce
- 3/4 cup hot water
- Pepper
- Salt

Directions:

1. Add all ingredients into the blender container. Secure the lid.
2. Start the blending at low speed, then quickly increase to highest speed and blend until smooth.
3. Serve and enjoy.

Nutritional Value (Amount per Serving):

- Calories 110
- Fat 8.3 g
- Carbohydrates 7.6 g
- Sugar 1.9 g
- Protein 2.9 g
- Cholesterol 0 mg

Perfect Artichoke Dip

Preparation Time: 5 minutes
Cooking Time: 1 minute
Serve: 4

Ingredients:

- 14 oz can artichoke hearts, drained
- 2 tbsp water
- 1 tsp chili powder
- 2 garlic cloves
- 1 tbsp lemon juice
- 2 tbsp olive oil
- 2 tbsp tahini
- 1/4 cup nutritional yeast
- 15 oz can chickpeas, drained
- Pepper
- Salt

Directions:

1. Add all ingredients into the blender container. Secure the lid.
2. Start the blending at low speed, then quickly increase to highest speed and blend for 1 minute or until getting the desired consistency.
3. Serve and enjoy.

Nutritional Value (Amount per Serving):

- Calories 301
- Fat 12.9 g
- Carbohydrates 36.1 g
- Sugar 1 g
- Protein 13 g
- Cholesterol 0 mg

Quick Olive Dip

Preparation Time: 5 minutes
Cooking Time: 1 minute
Serve: 8

Ingredients:

- 6 oz green olives, drained
- 16 oz cream cheese, softened
- 1/2 tsp garlic powder
- 1/2 tsp onion powder
- 1/2 cup mayonnaise

Directions:

1. Add all ingredients into the blender container. Secure the lid.
2. Start the blending at low speed, then quickly increase to highest speed and blend for 1 minute or until getting the desired consistency.
3. Serve and enjoy.

Nutritional Value (Amount per Serving):

- Calories 274
- Fat 26.1 g
- Carbohydrates 6.5 g
- Sugar 1.1 g
- Protein 4.7 g
- Cholesterol 66 mg

Roasted Pepper Hummus

Preparation Time: 5 minutes
Cooking Time: 1 minute
Serve: 8

Ingredients:

- 15 oz can chickpeas, drain
- 1 tsp ground cumin
- 4 garlic cloves
- 1 tbsp tahini
- 1/4 cup fresh lemon juice
- 1/2 cup roasted red peppers, drained
- 1/4 cup vegetable broth
- Pepper
- Salt

Directions:

1. Add all ingredients into the blender container. Secure the lid.
2. Start the blending at low speed, then quickly increase to highest speed and blend until smooth.
3. Serve and enjoy.

Nutritional Value (Amount per Serving):

- Calories 83
- Fat 1.8 g
- Carbohydrates 13.8 g
- Sugar 0.7 g
- Protein 3.4 g
- Cholesterol 0 mg

Spicy Chipotle Ranch Dip

Preparation Time: 5 minutes
Cooking Time: 1 minute
Serve: 4

Ingredients:

- 2 chipotle peppers in adobo sauce
- 3 tbsp water
- 1 garlic clove
- 1/2 tbsp fresh lime juice
- 1 tsp dried dill
- 1/2 tsp onion powder
- 1 1/2 tsp garlic powder
- 1/2 cup Greek yogurt
- 1/2 cup mayonnaise
- Pepper
- Salt

Directions:

1. Add all ingredients into the blender container. Secure the lid.
2. Start the blending at low speed, then quickly increase to highest speed and blend until smooth.
3. Serve and enjoy.

Nutritional Value (Amount per Serving):

- Calories 154
- Fat 10.6 g
- Carbohydrates 12.9 g
- Sugar 4.4 g
- Protein 3.1 g
- Cholesterol 9 mg

Easy Avocado Dip

Preparation Time: 5 minutes
Cooking Time: 1 minute
Serve: 6

Ingredients:

- 2 avocados, scoop out the flesh
- 1/4 tsp onion powder
- 1/2 cup Greek yogurt
- 1 lemon juice
- 1 cup fresh cilantro
- 2 garlic cloves
- Pepper
- Salt

Directions:

1. Add all ingredients into the blender container. Secure the lid.
2. Start the blending at low speed, then quickly increase to highest speed and blend until smooth.
3. Serve and enjoy.

Nutritional Value (Amount per Serving):

- Calories 154
- Fat 13.5 g
- Carbohydrates 7.1 g
- Sugar 1.2 g
- Protein 3.1 g
- Cholesterol 1 mg

Creamy Avocado Dip

Preparation Time: 5 minutes
Cooking Time: 1 minute
Serve: 6

Ingredients:

- 1 avocado, scoop out the flesh
- 1 lime juice
- 2 tbsp water
- 1 garlic clove
- 1/2 cup fresh cilantro
- 1/3 cup mayonnaise

Directions:

1. Add all ingredients into the blender container. Secure the lid.
2. Start the blending at low speed, then quickly increase to highest speed and blend until smooth.
3. Serve and enjoy.

Nutritional Value (Amount per Serving):

- Calories 122
- Fat 10.9 g
- Carbohydrates 6.8 g
- Sugar 1.2 g
- Protein 0.9 g
- Cholesterol 3 mg

Feta Red Pepper Dip

Preparation Time: 5 minutes
Cooking Time: 1 minute
Serve: 8

Ingredients:

- 1/2 cup can roasted red peppers, drained
- 8 oz feta cheese
- 1/3 cup extra-virgin olive oil
- 4 garlic cloves
- Pepper
- Salt

Directions:

1. Add all ingredients into the blender container. Secure the lid.
2. Start the blending at low speed, then quickly increase to highest speed and blend until smooth.
3. Serve and enjoy.

Nutritional Value (Amount per Serving):

- Calories 155
- Fat 14.6 g
- Carbohydrates 2.8 g
- Sugar 1.9 g
- Protein 4.3 g
- Cholesterol 25 mg

Flavorful Cranberry Salsa

Preparation Time: 5 minutes
Cooking Time: 1 minute
Serve: 8

Ingredients:

- 12 oz fresh cranberries
- 2 jalapeno peppers, chopped
- 1/4 cup fresh cilantro
- 1 tbsp orange zest
- 2 tbsp ginger, chopped
- 2 tbsp fresh lemon juice
- 1/2 cup sugar
- Pinch of salt

Directions:

1. Add all ingredients into the blender container. Secure the lid.
2. Start the blending at low speed, then quickly increase to highest speed and blend until getting chunky consistency.
3. Pour blended mixture into the bowl and place in the refrigerator for 5-6 hours.
4. Serve and enjoy.

Nutritional Value (Amount per Serving):

- Calories 78
- Fat 0.2 g
- Carbohydrates 17.9 g
- Sugar 14.3 g
- Protein 0.2 g
- Cholesterol 0 mg

Chapter 2: Soups & Salsas

Spicy Squash Soup

Preparation Time: 5 minutes
Cooking Time: 6 minutes
Serve: 4

Ingredients:

- 1 butternut squash, cut into chunks
- 1 potato, peel, cook, and chopped
- 1 onion, chopped
- 1 red chili, chopped
- 3 garlic cloves, peeled
- 3 cups vegetable stock
- Pepper
- Salt

Directions:

1. Add all ingredients into the blender container. Secure the lid.
2. Start the blending at low speed, then quickly increase to highest speed and blend for 6 minutes.
3. Serve and enjoy.

Nutritional Value (Amount per Serving):

- Calories 68
- Fat 0.2 g
- Carbohydrates 15.6 g
- Sugar 2.9 g
- Protein 2 g
- Cholesterol 0 mg

Potato Leek Soup

Preparation Time: 5 minutes
Cooking Time: 6 minutes
Serve: 4

Ingredients:

- 1 lb potatoes, peel, cooked, and chopped
- 1 onion, chopped
- 1 cup leek, chopped
- 3 cups vegetable stock
- 1/2 cup fresh cream
- Pepper
- Salt

Directions:

1. Add all ingredients into the blender container. Secure the lid.
2. Start the blending at low speed, then quickly increase to highest speed and blend for 6 minutes.
3. Serve and enjoy.

Nutritional Value (Amount per Serving):

- Calories 127
- Fat 2 g
- Carbohydrates 25.2 g
- Sugar 4.5 g
- Protein 3.1 g
- Cholesterol 6 mg

Creamy Asparagus Soup

Preparation Time: 5 minutes
Cooking Time: 6 minutes
Serve: 4

Ingredients:

- 1 lb asparagus, cooked and chopped
- 2 garlic cloves
- 1 onion, diced
- 3 1/4 cups vegetable stock
- 1 tbsp olive oil
- 1 tbsp fresh lemon juice
- 1 leek, sliced
- Pepper
- Salt

Directions:

1. Add all ingredients into the blender container. Secure the lid.
2. Start the blending at low speed, then quickly increase to highest speed and blend for 6 minutes.
3. Serve and enjoy.

Nutritional Value (Amount per Serving):

- Calories 85
- Fat 3.9 g
- Carbohydrates 11.5 g
- Sugar 4.8 g
- Protein 3.6 g
- Cholesterol 0 mg

Delicious Cranberry Salsa

Preparation Time: 5 minutes
Cooking Time: 1 minute
Serve: 8

Ingredients:

- 12 oz cranberries
- 2 jalapeno pepper, chopped
- 1/4 cup cilantro
- 1 tbsp lemon zest
- 1 1/2 tbsp ginger, chopped
- 2 tbsp lime juice
- 1/2 cup sugar

Directions:

1. Add all ingredients into the blender container. Secure the lid.
2. Start the blending at low speed, then slowly increase speed to variable 3 and blend for 15-20 seconds or until getting the desired consistency.
3. Serve and enjoy.

Nutritional Value (Amount per Serving):

- Calories 78
- Fat 0.1 g
- Carbohydrates 18.4 g
- Sugar 14.2 g
- Protein 0.2 g
- Cholesterol 0 mg

Creamy Squash Soup

Preparation Time: 5 minutes
Cooking Time: 6 minutes
Serve: 6

Ingredients:

- 6 cups butternut squash, peel, cook, and cubed
- 2 tsp thyme
- 1/4 cup heavy cream
- 3 cups vegetable stock
- 1 onion, chopped
- 1/8 tsp nutmeg
- 2 tbsp olive oil
- 1/8 tsp cayenne
- Pepper
- Salt

Directions:

1. Add all ingredients into the blender container. Secure the lid.
2. Start the blending at low speed, then quickly increase to highest speed and blend for 6 minutes.
3. Serve and enjoy.

Nutritional Value (Amount per Serving):

- Calories 132
- Fat 6.8 g
- Carbohydrates 18.9 g
- Sugar 4.2 g
- Protein 1.9 g
- Cholesterol 7 mg

Tasty Garden Salsa

Preparation Time: 5 minutes
Cooking Time: 1 minute
Serve: 8

Ingredients:

- 5 tomatoes, halved
- 2 garlic cloves
- 1 lime juice
- 1 jalapeno pepper
- 1/2 onion
- 1/2 tsp sugar
- Pepper
- Salt

Directions:

1. Add all ingredients into the blender container. Secure the lid.
2. Start the blending at low speed, then slowly increase speed to variable 3 and blend for 15-20 seconds or until getting the desired consistency.
3. Serve and enjoy.

Nutritional Value (Amount per Serving):

- Calories 21
- Fat 0.2 g
- Carbohydrates 4.7 g
- Sugar 2.7 g
- Protein 0.9 g
- Cholesterol 0 mg

Strawberry Salsa

Preparation Time: 5 minutes
Cooking Time: 1 minute
Serve: 4

Ingredients:

- 1 cup strawberries
- 1/4 cup cilantro
- 1 lime juice
- 1 jalapeno pepper
- 1/4 onion

Directions:

1. Add all ingredients into the blender container. Secure the lid.
2. Start the blending at low speed, then slowly increase speed to variable 3 and blend for 15-20 seconds or until getting chunky consistency.
3. Serve and enjoy.

Nutritional Value (Amount per Serving):

- Calories 18
- Fat 0.2 g
- Carbohydrates 4.6 g
- Sugar 2.4 g
- Protein 0.4 g
- Cholesterol 0 mg

Spicy Chipotle Salsa

Preparation Time: 5 minutes
Cooking Time: 1 minute
Serve: 8

Ingredients:

- 10 oz can tomatoes with green chilies
- 14 oz can tomatoes, diced
- 4 garlic cloves
- 1 small onion, diced
- 1 tsp ground cumin
- 1 tbsp lime juice
- 2 chipotle peppers
- 1/2 cup cilantro
- Salt

Directions:

1. Add all ingredients into the blender container. Secure the lid.
2. Start the blending at low speed, then slowly increase speed to variable 3 and blend for 15-20 seconds or until getting the desired consistency.
3. Serve and enjoy.

Nutritional Value (Amount per Serving):

- Calories 29
- Fat 0.1 g
- Carbohydrates 6.8 g
- Sugar 2.8 g
- Protein 1.2 g
- Cholesterol 0 mg

Tomatillo Pineapple Salsa

Preparation Time: 5 minutes
Cooking Time: 1 minute
Serve: 8

Ingredients:

- 1 cup pineapple, diced
- 1 jalapeno pepper
- 1 lb tomatillos, husks removed & chopped
- 1 cup water
- 1/2 lime juice
- 1/2 cup cilantro
- 4.5 green chilies, diced
- 1/2 onion, chopped
- 1/2 tsp salt

Directions:

1. Add all ingredients into the blender container. Secure the lid.
2. Start the blending at low speed, then slowly increase speed to variable 3 and blend for 15-20 seconds or until getting the desired consistency.
3. Serve and enjoy.

Nutritional Value (Amount per Serving):

- Calories 34
- Fat 0.7 g
- Carbohydrates 7.2 g
- Sugar 2.6 g
- Protein 0.8 g
- Cholesterol 0 mg

Mango Salsa

Preparation Time: 5 minutes
Cooking Time: 1 minute
Serve: 8

Ingredients:

- 1 1/2 cups mangoes, diced
- 1/3 cup green onion, chopped
- 1 bell pepper, diced
- 1 lime juice
- 1 jalapeno pepper, diced
- 1/2 cup cilantro
- Salt

Directions:

1. Add all ingredients into the blender container. Secure the lid.
2. Start the blending at low speed, then slowly increase speed to variable 3 and blend for 15-20 seconds or until getting the desired consistency.
3. Serve and enjoy.

Nutritional Value (Amount per Serving):

- Calories 25
- Fat 0.2 g
- Carbohydrates 6.7 g
- Sugar 5.2 g
- Protein 0.5 g
- Cholesterol 0 mg

Berry Salsa

Preparation Time: 5 minutes
Cooking Time: 1 minute
Serve: 8

Ingredients:

- 8 strawberries
- 2 cups blueberries
- 1 lime juice
- 1 jalapeno pepper
- 1/4 cup cilantro
- Salt

Directions:

1. Add all ingredients into the blender container. Secure the lid.
2. Start the blending at low speed, then slowly increase speed to variable 3 and blend for 15-20 seconds or until getting the desired consistency.
3. Serve and enjoy.

Nutritional Value (Amount per Serving):

- Calories 25
- Fat 0.2 g
- Carbohydrates 6.3 g
- Sugar 4.3 g
- Protein 0.4 g
- Cholesterol 0 mg

Cauliflower Soup

Preparation Time: 5 minutes
Cooking Time: 6 minutes
Serve: 4

Ingredients:

- 2 cups cauliflower florets, boiled & drained
- 1 tsp pumpkin pie spice
- 1 onion, chopped
- 5 cups vegetable broth
- 3 tbsp olive oil
- Pepper
- Salt

Directions:

1. Add all ingredients into the blender container. Secure the lid.
2. Start the blending at low speed, then quickly increase to highest speed and blend for 6 minutes.
3. Serve and enjoy.

Nutritional Value (Amount per Serving):

- Calories 163
- Fat 12.3 g
- Carbohydrates 6.7 g
- Sugar 3.3 g
- Protein 7.4 g
- Cholesterol 0 mg

Chapter 3: Dressing, Sauces & Spreads

Enchilada Sauce

Preparation Time: 10 minutes
Cooking Time: 1 minute
Serve: 4

Ingredients:

- 8 oz can tomato sauce
- 1/4 tsp cayenne
- 1/4 tsp garlic powder
- 1/4 tsp ground cumin
- 1 cup water
- 2 tbsp chili powder
- 2 tbsp flour
- 1/4 cup olive oil
- Pepper
- Salt

Directions:

1. Add all ingredients into the blender container. Secure the lid.
2. Start the blending at low speed, then quickly increase to highest speed and blend for 1 minute or until smooth.
3. Serve and enjoy.

Nutritional Value (Amount per Serving):

- Calories 149
- Fat 13.4 g
- Carbohydrates 8.4 g
- Sugar 2.7 g
- Protein 1.7 g
- Cholesterol 0 mg

Low-carb BBQ Sauce

Preparation Time: 10 minutes
Cooking Time: 1 minute
Serve: 4

Ingredients:

- 6 oz can tomato paste
- 1 tsp Dijon mustard
- 1/2 tsp chipotle powder
- 3/4 tsp paprika
- 1 tsp garlic powder
- 1 tbsp onion powder
- 1/2 cup Swerve
- 2 tbsp water
- 1/4 cup vinegar
- 1 tsp salt

Directions:

1. Add all ingredients into the blender container. Secure the lid.
2. Start the blending at low speed, then quickly increase to highest speed and blend for 1 minute or until smooth.
3. Serve and enjoy.

Nutritional Value (Amount per Serving):

- Calories 49
- Fat 0.4 g
- Carbohydrates 10.6 g
- Sugar 6.1 g
- Protein 2.3 g
- Cholesterol 0 mg

Mango Lemon Dressing

Preparation Time: 10 minutes
Cooking Time: 1 minute
Serve: 6

Ingredients:

- 1 cup mango, diced
- 1/2 tsp garlic powder
- 1/2 tsp ground cumin
- 1/4 cup cilantro
- 1 tbsp olive oil
- 1 tbsp vinegar
- 1 lemon juice
- Salt

Directions:

1. Add all ingredients into the blender container. Secure the lid.
2. Start the blending at low speed, then quickly increase to highest speed and blend for 1 minute or until smooth.
3. Serve and enjoy.

Nutritional Value (Amount per Serving):

- Calories 41
- Fat 2.5 g
- Carbohydrates 4.6 g
- Sugar 4 g
- Protein 0.4 g
- Cholesterol 0 mg

Chickpea Pepper Spread

Preparation Time: 10 minutes
Cooking Time: 1 minute
Serve: 8

Ingredients:

- 14.5 oz can chickpeas, drained
- 1 tbsp olive oil
- 1/2 tsp paprika
- 1 tbsp vinegar
- 4 oz can roasted red peppers, drained
- Pepper
- Salt

Directions:

1. Add all ingredients into the blender container. Secure the lid.
2. Start the blending at low speed, then quickly increase to highest speed and blend for 1 minute or until smooth & creamy.
3. Serve and enjoy.

Nutritional Value (Amount per Serving):

- Calories 83
- Fat 2.5 g
- Carbohydrates 12.7 g
- Sugar 0.6 g
- Protein 2.7 g
- Cholesterol 0 mg

Flavorful Peanut Sauce

Preparation Time: 10 minutes
Cooking Time: 1 minute
Serve: 8

Ingredients:

- 1/2 cup creamy peanut butter
- 3 tbsp water
- 1 tsp sriracha sauce
- 1/2 lemon juice
- 1 tbsp soy sauce
- 2 garlic cloves
- 1/2 tbsp fresh ginger, chopped

Directions:

1. Add all ingredients into the blender container. Secure the lid.
2. Start the blending at low speed, then quickly increase to highest speed and blend for 1 minute or until smooth.
3. Serve and enjoy.

Nutritional Value (Amount per Serving):

- Calories 99
- Fat 8.2 g
- Carbohydrates 3.9 g
- Sugar 1.6 g
- Protein 4.3 g
- Cholesterol 0 mg

Creamy Avocado Dressing

Preparation Time: 10 minutes
Cooking Time: 1 minute
Serve: 4

Ingredients:

- 1 avocado, scoop out the flesh
- 1 garlic clove
- 1 lemon juice
- 2 tbsp water
- 1/4 cup olive oil
- 1/2 cup cilantro
- Pepper
- Salt

Directions:

1. Add all ingredients into the blender container. Secure the lid.
2. Start the blending at low speed, then quickly increase to highest speed and blend for 1 minute or until smooth.
3. Serve and enjoy.

Nutritional Value (Amount per Serving):

- Calories 215
- Fat 22.5 g
- Carbohydrates 4.9 g
- Sugar 0.5 g
- Protein 1.1 g
- Cholesterol 0 mg

Avocado Sandwich Spread

Preparation Time: 10 minutes
Cooking Time: 1 minute
Serve: 2

Ingredients:

- 1 avocado, scoop out the flesh
- 1 lime juice
- 2 tbsp green onion
- 1/4 cup cilantro
- 1/4 tsp paprika
- 14.5 oz can chickpeas, drained
- Pepper
- Salt

Directions:

1. Add all ingredients into the blender container. Secure the lid.
2. Start the blending at low speed, then quickly increase to highest speed and blend for 1 minute or until getting a chunky consistency.
3. Serve and enjoy.

Nutritional Value (Amount per Serving):

- Calories 458
- Fat 22 g
- Carbohydrates 57.6 g
- Sugar 1.1 g
- Protein 12.4 g
- Cholesterol 0 mg

Classic Caesar Dressing

Preparation Time: 10 minutes
Cooking Time: 1 minute
Serve: 4

Ingredients:

- 1/2 cup olive oil
- 1 tsp Dijon mustard
- 2 tbsp fresh lime juice
- 1/3 cup parmesan cheese, grated
- 2 egg yolks
- 1 garlic clove
- 4 anchovy fillets, drained
- Pepper
- Salt

Directions:

1. Add all ingredients into the blender container. Secure the lid.
2. Start the blending at low speed, then quickly increase to highest speed and blend for 1 minute or until smooth.
3. Serve and enjoy.

Nutritional Value (Amount per Serving):

- Calories 266
- Fat 28.4 g
- Carbohydrates 2.6 g
- Sugar 0.4 g
- Protein 3.5 g
- Cholesterol 110 mg

Creamy Tomatillo Dressing

Preparation Time: 10 minutes
Cooking Time: 1 minute
Serve: 16

Ingredients:

- 2 tomatillo, husked & chopped
- 1 jalapeno pepper, diced
- 1 lemon juice
- 1 garlic clove
- 1/2 cup cilantro
- 1 cup mayonnaise
- 1 cup buttermilk
- 1 packet ranch seasoning mix

Directions:

1. Add all ingredients into the blender container. Secure the lid.
2. Start the blending at low speed, then quickly increase to highest speed and blend for 1 minute or until smooth.
3. Serve and enjoy.

Nutritional Value (Amount per Serving):

- Calories 66
- Fat 5.1 g
- Carbohydrates 4.7 g
- Sugar 1.8 g
- Protein 0.7 g
- Cholesterol 4 mg

Southwest Dressing

Preparation Time: 10 minutes
Cooking Time: 1 minute
Serve: 8

Ingredients:

- 1/4 tsp chipotle powder
- 1/2 tsp paprika
- 1/2 tsp dill
- 1 tsp ground cumin
- 1 tsp onion powder
- 1 tsp garlic powder
- 1 1/2 tsp chili powder
- 1/4 cup fresh lemon juice
- 1 cup mayonnaise
- Salt

Directions:

1. Add all ingredients into the blender container. Secure the lid.
2. Start the blending at low speed, then quickly increase to highest speed and blend for 1 minute or until smooth.
3. Serve and enjoy.

Nutritional Value (Amount per Serving):

- Calories 138
- Fat 11.8 g
- Carbohydrates 8.3 g
- Sugar 2.4 g
- Protein 0.6 g
- Cholesterol 9 mg

Mango Mustard Sauce

Preparation Time: 10 minutes
Cooking Time: 1 minute
Serve: 4

Ingredients:

- 1/2 cup mango, chopped
- 1 tbsp fresh lemon juice
- 1 tsp red chili flakes
- 2 1/2 tbsp Dijon mustard
- 1/4 cup mayonnaise
- Salt

Directions:

1. Add all ingredients into the blender container. Secure the lid.
2. Start the blending at low speed, then quickly increase to highest speed and blend for 1 minute or until smooth.
3. Serve and enjoy.

Nutritional Value (Amount per Serving):

- Calories 77
- Fat 5.4 g
- Carbohydrates 7.2 g
- Sugar 3.9 g
- Protein 0.8 g
- Cholesterol 4 mg

Chimichurri Sauce

Preparation Time: 10 minutes
Cooking Time: 1 minute
Serve: 8

Ingredients:

- 1 jalapeno pepper
- 1 small onion, quartered
- 4 garlic cloves
- 2 tsp dried oregano
- 1/2 cup fresh cilantro
- 1/2 cup fresh parsley
- 1/2 cup vinegar
- 1/2 cup extra-virgin olive oil
- Pepper
- Salt

Directions:

1. Add all ingredients into the blender container. Secure the lid.
2. Start the blending at low speed, then quickly increase to highest speed and blend for 1 minute or until smooth.
3. Serve and enjoy.

Nutritional Value (Amount per Serving):

- Calories 120
- Fat 12.7 g
- Carbohydrates 2.1 g
- Sugar 0.6 g
- Protein 0.4 g
- Cholesterol 0 mg

Creamy Avocado Sauce

Preparation Time: 10 minutes
Cooking Time: 1 minute
Serve: 8

Ingredients:

- 1 avocado, scoop out the flesh
- 2 tbsp fresh lemon juice
- 4 oz sour cream
- 1/4 tsp garlic powder
- Pepper
- Salt

Directions:

1. Add all ingredients into the blender container. Secure the lid.
2. Start the blending at low speed, then quickly increase to highest speed and blend for 1 minute or until smooth.
3. Serve and enjoy.

Nutritional Value (Amount per Serving):

- Calories 83
- Fat 7.9 g
- Carbohydrates 2.9 g
- Sugar 0.3 g
- Protein 1 g
- Cholesterol 6 mg

Honey Mustard Dressing

Preparation Time: 10 minutes
Cooking Time: 1 minute
Serve: 8

Ingredients:

- 3/4 cup olive oil
- 1/3 cup vinegar
- 2 tbsp lime juice
- 1 garlic clove
- 1/4 cup Dijon mustard
- 1/4 cup honey
- Salt

Directions:

1. Add all ingredients into the blender container. Secure the lid.
2. Start the blending at low speed, then quickly increase to highest speed and blend for 1 minute or until smooth.
3. Serve and enjoy.

Nutritional Value (Amount per Serving):

- Calories 205
- Fat 19.2 g
- Carbohydrates 10.3 g
- Sugar 9 g
- Protein 0.4 g
- Cholesterol 0 mg

Zesty Chipotle Ranch Dressing

Preparation Time: 10 minutes
Cooking Time: 1 minute
Serve: 6

Ingredients:

- 1 chipotle pepper
- 1/2 tsp dill
- 1/4 tsp onion powder
- 1/2 tsp garlic powder
- 2 tbsp cilantro
- 1 tbsp lime juice
- 1/4 cup buttermilk
- 1/4 cup sour cream
- 1/2 cup mayonnaise
- Pepper
- Salt

Directions:

1. Add all ingredients into the blender container. Secure the lid.
2. Start the blending at low speed, then quickly increase to highest speed and blend for 1 minute or until smooth.
3. Serve and enjoy.

Nutritional Value (Amount per Serving):

- Calories 111
- Fat 8.7 g
- Carbohydrates 8.1 g
- Sugar 2.8 g
- Protein 1.3 g
- Cholesterol 10 mg

Cheese Pepper Spread

Preparation Time: 10 minutes
Cooking Time: 1 minute
Serve: 20

Ingredients:

- 1 cup can roasted red peppers, drained
- 1/4 tsp red chili flakes
- 1 tsp lime juice
- 8 oz cream cheese
- 1 garlic clove
- 1/2 tsp dried basil
- Pepper
- Salt

Directions:

1. Add all ingredients into the blender container. Secure the lid.
2. Start the blending at low speed, then quickly increase to highest speed and blend for 1 minute or until smooth & creamy.
3. Serve and enjoy.

Nutritional Value (Amount per Serving):

- Calories 45
- Fat 4.1 g
- Carbohydrates 1.4 g
- Sugar 0.6 g
- Protein 1 g
- Cholesterol 12 mg

Vegan Greek Dressing

Preparation Time: 10 minutes
Cooking Time: 1 minute
Serve: 8

Ingredients:

- 1 cup olive oil
- 1/4 tsp red chili flakes
- 1/4 cup parsley
- 1 tbsp Dijon mustard
- 1 tsp dried basil
- 1 tsp dried oregano
- 2 garlic cloves
- 1/3 cup water
- 1/2 cup vinegar
- Pepper
- Salt

Directions:

1. Add all ingredients into the blender container. Secure the lid.
2. Start the blending at low speed, then quickly increase to highest speed and blend for 1 minute or until smooth.
3. Serve and enjoy.

Nutritional Value (Amount per Serving):

- Calories 223
- Fat 25.3 g
- Carbohydrates 0.7 g
- Sugar 0.1 g
- Protein 0.2 g
- Cholesterol 0 mg

Easy Hollandaise Sauce

Preparation Time: 10 minutes
Cooking Time: 1 minute
Serve: 12

Ingredients:

- 3 egg yolks
- 1/2 cup butter, melted
- 1 tbsp vinegar
- 3/4 tsp dry mustard
- Pepper
- Salt

Directions:

1. Add all ingredients into the blender container. Secure the lid.
2. Start the blending at low speed, then quickly increase to highest speed and blend for 1 minute or until thick & fluffy.
3. Serve and enjoy.

Nutritional Value (Amount per Serving):

- Calories 83
- Fat 8.9 g
- Carbohydrates 0.3 g
- Sugar 0.1 g
- Protein 0.8 g
- Cholesterol 73 mg

Chapter 4: Desserts

Mango Sorbet

Preparation Time: 5 minutes
Cooking Time: 1 minute
Serve: 5

Ingredients:

- 4 cups mangoes, diced
- 3 cups ice cubes
- 1 cup sugar
- 1 tsp lime juice

Directions:

1. Add all ingredients into the blender container. Secure the lid.
2. Start the blending at low speed, then slowly increase to the highest speed and blend for 5 minutes or until smooth.
3. Serve and enjoy.

Nutritional Value (Amount per Serving):

- Calories 229
- Fat 0.5 g
- Carbohydrates 60.5 g
- Sugar 58.2 g
- Protein 1.1 g
- Cholesterol 0 mg

Blueberry Ice Cream

Preparation Time: 5 minutes
Cooking Time: 1 minute
Serve: 4

Ingredients:

- 1 cup heavy whipping cream
- 1 1/2 cups frozen blueberries
- 4 tbsp erythritol

Directions:

1. Add all ingredients into the blender container. Secure the lid.
2. Start the blending at low speed, then slowly increase to highest speed and blend for 1 minute or until smooth.
3. Pour into the container and place in the refrigerator for 4 hours.
4. Serve and enjoy.

Nutritional Value (Amount per Serving):

- Calories 135
- Fat 11.3 g
- Carbohydrates 23.7 g
- Sugar 20.4 g
- Protein 1 g
- Cholesterol 41 mg

Strawberry Banana Sorbet

Preparation Time: 5 minutes
Cooking Time: 1 minute
Serve: 6

Ingredients:

- 1/2 lb frozen strawberry
- 1/2 lb frozen banana
- 1/3 cup honey
- 3 tbsp fresh lemon juice

Directions:

1. Add all ingredients into the blender container. Secure the lid.
2. Start the blending at low speed, then slowly increase to highest speed and blend for 1 minute or until smooth.
3. Pour into the container and place in the refrigerator for 3 hours.
4. Serve and enjoy.

Nutritional Value (Amount per Serving):

- Calories 106
- Fat 0.7 g
- Carbohydrates 25.2 g
- Sugar 21.9 g
- Protein 1.2 g
- Cholesterol 3 mg

Perfect Pineapple Ice Cream

Preparation Time: 5 minutes
Cooking Time: 5 minutes
Serve: 6

Ingredients:

- 20 oz can crushed pineapple
- 1/2 cup heavy cream
- 1 1/2 cups pineapple juice

Directions:

1. Add all ingredients into the blender container. Secure the lid.
2. Start the blending at low speed, then slowly increase to the highest speed and blend for 5 minutes or until smooth.
3. Pour into the container and place in the refrigerator for 4 hours.
4. Serve and enjoy.

Nutritional Value (Amount per Serving):

- Calories 118
- Fat 3.8 g
- Carbohydrates 20.9 g
- Sugar 15.7 g
- Protein 0.8 g
- Cholesterol 14 mg

Easy Strawberry Ice Cream

Preparation Time: 5 minutes
Cooking Time: 1 minute
Serve: 1

Ingredients:

- 10 frozen strawberries
- 1/2 tsp vanilla
- 1 scoop vanilla protein powder
- 1/2 frozen banana
- 1/4 cup full-fat coconut milk

Directions:

1. Add all ingredients into the blender container. Secure the lid.
2. Start the blending at low speed, then slowly increase to highest speed and blend for 1 minute or until smooth.
3. Serve and enjoy.

Nutritional Value (Amount per Serving):

- Calories 688
- Fat 4.3 g
- Carbohydrates 142.6 g
- Sugar 98 g
- Protein 24.8 g
- Cholesterol 15 mg

Pumpkin Mousse

Preparation Time: 5 minutes
Cooking Time: 1 minute
Serve: 10

Ingredients:

- 15 oz can pumpkin puree
- 3/4 cup heavy cream
- 2 tbsp pumpkin spice
- 2 tsp vanilla
- 1/2 cup Swerve
- 12 oz cream cheese, softened

Directions:

1. Add all ingredients into the blender container. Secure the lid.
2. Start the blending at low speed, then slowly increase to highest speed and blend for 1 minute or until smooth.
3. Pour into the container and place in the refrigerator for 2 hours.
4. Serve and enjoy.

Nutritional Value (Amount per Serving):

- Calories 219
- Fat 15.3 g
- Carbohydrates 17.1 g
- Sugar 6.3 g
- Protein 4.3 g
- Cholesterol 50 mg

Fluffy Strawberry Mousse

Preparation Time: 5 minutes
Cooking Time: 1 minute
Serve: 10

Ingredients:

- 1 cup strawberries
- 3 oz strawberry jello
- 1 cup hot water
- 3 tbsp sugar
- 5 tbsp mascarpone cheese
- 2 cups heavy whipping cream

Directions:

1. Add all ingredients into the blender container. Secure the lid.
2. Start the blending at low speed, then slowly increase to highest speed and blend for 1 minute or until smooth.
3. Pour into the container and place in the refrigerator for 6 hours.
4. Serve and enjoy.

Nutritional Value (Amount per Serving):

- Calories 120
- Fat 9.9 g
- Carbohydrates 6.8 g
- Sugar 5.5 g
- Protein 1.6 g
- Cholesterol 37 mg

Chocolate Mousse

Preparation Time: 5 minutes
Cooking Time: 1 minute
Serve: 4

Ingredients:

- 6 oz chocolate, melted
- 1/2 tsp vanilla
- 3 avocados, scoop out the flesh
- 1/2 cup cocoa powder
- 3 tbsp coconut oil, melted

Directions:

1. Add all ingredients into the blender container. Secure the lid.
2. Start the blending at low speed, then slowly increase to highest speed and blend for 1 minute or until smooth.
3. Pour into the container and place in the refrigerator for 1 hour.
4. Serve and enjoy.

Nutritional Value (Amount per Serving):

- Calories 648
- Fat 53.6 g
- Carbohydrates 44.2 g
- Sugar 22.9 g
- Protein 8.1 g
- Cholesterol 10 mg

Orange Pineapple Sorbet

Preparation Time: 5 minutes
Cooking Time: 1 minute
Serve: 4

Ingredients:

- 1/2 orange zest
- 3 cups frozen pineapple chunks

Directions:

1. Add all ingredients into the blender container. Secure the lid.
2. Start the blending at low speed, then slowly increase to highest speed and blend for 1 minute or until smooth.
3. Pour into the container and place in the refrigerator for 4 hours.
4. Serve and enjoy.

Nutritional Value (Amount per Serving):

- Calories 159
- Fat 0.2 g
- Carbohydrates 41 g
- Sugar 38.8 g
- Protein 0.8 g
- Cholesterol 0 mg

Yummy Blueberry Yogurt

Preparation Time: 5 minutes
Cooking Time: 1 minute
Serve: 2

Ingredients:

- 1 cup frozen blueberries
- 1 tsp vanilla
- 2 tbsp maple syrup
- 1 1/2 cups almond milk yogurt
- Pinch of salt

Directions:

1. Add all ingredients into the blender container. Secure the lid.
2. Start the blending at low speed, then slowly increase to highest speed and blend for 1 minute or until smooth.
3. Serve and enjoy.

Nutritional Value (Amount per Serving):

- Calories 212
- Fat 4.8 g
- Carbohydrates 42.2 g
- Sugar 32.9 g
- Protein 2.8 g
- Cholesterol 0 mg

Strawberry Cheesecake Ice Cream

Preparation Time: 5 minutes
Cooking Time: 1 minute
Serve: 2

Ingredients:

- 1 cup frozen strawberries
- 6 drops liquid stevia
- 1 tbsp cream cheese
- 1/4 cup greek yogurt
- 3/4 cup almond milk

Directions:

1. Add all ingredients into the blender container. Secure the lid.
2. Start the blending at low speed, then slowly increase to highest speed and blend for 1 minute or until smooth.
3. Serve and enjoy.

Nutritional Value (Amount per Serving):

- Calories 268
- Fat 23.7 g
- Carbohydrates 12.6 g
- Sugar 8.5 g
- Protein 5 g
- Cholesterol 7 mg

Pineapple Mango Sorbet

Preparation Time: 5 minutes
Cooking Time: 1 minute
Serve: 4

Ingredients:

- 2 cups frozen pineapple
- 2 cups frozen mango
- 1 tbsp maple syrup

Directions:

1. Add all ingredients into the blender container. Secure the lid.
2. Start the blending at low speed, then slowly increase to highest speed and blend for 1 minute or until smooth.
3. Serve and enjoy.

Nutritional Value (Amount per Serving):

- Calories 178
- Fat 2.6 g
- Carbohydrates 37.3 g
- Sugar 32.7 g
- Protein 2.5 g
- Cholesterol 10 mg

Coconut Popsicles

Preparation Time: 5 minutes
Cooking Time: 1 minute
Serve: 4

Ingredients:

- 14 oz coconut milk
- 1 banana
- 1 tbsp maple syrup

Directions:

1. Add all ingredients into the blender container. Secure the lid.
2. Start the blending at low speed, then slowly increase to highest speed and blend for 1 minute or until smooth.
3. Pour into the popsicle molds and place in refrigerator until set.
4. Serve and enjoy.

Nutritional Value (Amount per Serving):

- Calories 268
- Fat 23.8 g
- Carbohydrates 15.6 g
- Sugar 9.9 g
- Protein 2.6 g
- Cholesterol 0 mg

Easy Lemon Curd

Preparation Time: 5 minutes
Cooking Time: 5 minutes
Serve: 4

Ingredients:

- 5 eggs
- 1/2 cup butter, cut into chunks
- 1 1/2 cups sugar
- 1/2 cup lemon juice
- 1/8 tsp salt

Directions:

1. Add all ingredients into the blender container. Secure the lid.
2. Start the blending at low speed, then slowly increase to the highest speed and blend for 5 minutes.
3. Pour into the container and place in the refrigerator for 2 hours.
4. Serve and enjoy.

Nutritional Value (Amount per Serving):

- Calories 571
- Fat 28.7 g
- Carbohydrates 76.1 g
- Sugar 76.1 g
- Protein 7.4 g
- Cholesterol 266 mg

Coconut Cherry Popsicles

Preparation Time: 5 minutes
Cooking Time: 1 minute
Serve: 10

Ingredients:

- 14 oz can full-fat coconut milk
- 1 tsp maple syrup
- 2 cups fresh cherries, pitted

Directions:

1. Add all ingredients into the blender container. Secure the lid.
2. Start the blending at low speed, then slowly increase to highest speed and blend for 1 minute or until smooth.
3. Pour into the popsicle molds and place in refrigerator until set.
4. Serve and enjoy.

Nutritional Value (Amount per Serving):

- Calories 92
- Fat 7.3 g
- Carbohydrates 5.8 g
- Sugar 1 g
- Protein 0.7 g
- Cholesterol 0 mg

Easy Cherry Sorbet

Preparation Time: 5 minutes
Cooking Time: 1 minute
Serve: 6

Ingredients:

- 1 lb frozen cherries, pitted
- 1 tsp fresh lemon juice
- 1 cup sugar

Directions:

1. Add all ingredients into the blender container. Secure the lid.
2. Start the blending at low speed, then slowly increase to highest speed and blend for 1 minute or until smooth.
3. Pour into the container and place in the refrigerator for 5 hours.
4. Serve and enjoy.

Nutritional Value (Amount per Serving):

- Calories 160
- Fat 0.3 g
- Carbohydrates 41.7 g
- Sugar 40.2 g
- Protein 0.7 g
- Cholesterol 0 mg

Easy Pumpkin Mousse

Preparation Time: 5 minutes
Cooking Time: 1 minute
Serve: 4

Ingredients:

- 1/2 cup pumpkin puree
- 1 tsp vanilla
- 1 tbsp pumpkin pie spice
- 1/4 cup maple syrup
- 1 cup coconut cream
- Pinch of salt

Directions:

1. Add all ingredients into the blender container. Secure the lid.
2. Start the blending at low speed, then slowly increase to highest speed and blend for 1 minute or until smooth.
3. Pour into the container and place in the refrigerator for 2 hours.
4. Serve and enjoy.

Nutritional Value (Amount per Serving):

- Calories 208
- Fat 14.6 g
- Carbohydrates 20.1 g
- Sugar 15 g
- Protein 1.8 g
- Cholesterol 0 mg

Peach Ice Cream

Preparation Time: 5 minutes
Cooking Time: 1 minute
Serve: 4

Ingredients:

- 3 cups frozen peach slices
- 2 tbsp honey
- 1 1/2 cups almond milk

Directions:

1. Add all ingredients into the blender container. Secure the lid.
2. Start the blending at low speed, then slowly increase to highest speed and blend for 1 minute or until smooth.
3. Pour into the container and place in the refrigerator for 4 hours.
4. Serve and enjoy.

Nutritional Value (Amount per Serving):

- Calories 415
- Fat 21.7 g
- Carbohydrates 58.6 g
- Sugar 53.2 g
- Protein 3.3 g
- Cholesterol 0 mg

Nutella Banana Ice Cream

Preparation Time: 5 minutes
Cooking Time: 1 minute
Serve: 4

Ingredients:

- 4 frozen banana
- 1/2 cup Nutella

Directions:

1. Add all ingredients into the blender container. Secure the lid.
2. Start the blending at low speed, then slowly increase to highest speed and blend for 1 minute or until smooth.
3. Pour into the container and place in the refrigerator for 2 hours.
4. Serve and enjoy.

Nutritional Value (Amount per Serving):

- Calories 135
- Fat 3.4 g
- Carbohydrates 22.9 g
- Sugar 17.5 g
- Protein 3.3 g
- Cholesterol 10 mg

Raspberry Sorbet

Preparation Time: 5 minutes
Cooking Time: 1 minute
Serve: 2

Ingredients:

- 1/2 cup frozen cherries, pitted
- 1 1/3 cups frozen raspberries
- 1 frozen banana
- 2/3 cup almond milk

Directions:

1. Add all ingredients into the blender container. Secure the lid.
2. Start the blending at low speed, then slowly increase to highest speed and blend for 1 minute or until smooth.
3. Serve and enjoy.

Nutritional Value (Amount per Serving):

- Calories 429
- Fat 20.5 g
- Carbohydrates 62.3 g
- Sugar 49.9 g
- Protein 4.9 g
- Cholesterol 5 mg

Raspberry Mousse

Preparation Time: 5 minutes
Cooking Time: 1 minute
Serve: 2

Ingredients:

- 1 cup frozen raspberries
- 1 tbsp almond milk
- 1 frozen banana
- 1 avocado, scoop out the flesh

Directions:

1. Add all ingredients into the blender container. Secure the lid.
2. Start the blending at low speed, then slowly increase to highest speed and blend for 1 minute or until smooth.
3. Pour into the container and place in the refrigerator for 1 hour.
4. Serve and enjoy.

Nutritional Value (Amount per Serving):

- Calories 351
- Fat 21.6 g
- Carbohydrates 41.8 g
- Sugar 28 g
- Protein 3 g
- Cholesterol 0 mg

Blueberry Sorbet

Preparation Time: 5 minutes
Cooking Time: 1 minute
Serve: 4

Ingredients:

- 4 cups frozen blueberries
- 1/2 cup water
- 2 tbsp honey

Directions:

1. Add all ingredients into the blender container. Secure the lid.
2. Start the blending at low speed, then slowly increase to highest speed and blend for 1 minute or until smooth.
3. Pour into the container and place in the refrigerator for 4 hours.
4. Serve and enjoy.

Nutritional Value (Amount per Serving):

- Calories 115
- Fat 0.5 g
- Carbohydrates 29.7 g
- Sugar 23 g
- Protein 1.1 g
- Cholesterol 0 mg

Chapter 5: Drinks

Banana Coffee Smoothie

Preparation Time: 5 minutes
Cooking Time: 1 minute
Serve: 2

Ingredients:

- 1 cup brewed coffee
- 1 tbsp cocoa powder
- 1 cup milk
- 1 tbsp almond butter
- 1 banana

Directions:

1. Add all ingredients into the blender container. Secure the lid.
2. Start the blending on low speed, then quickly increase to highest speed and blend for 1 minute or until smooth.
3. Serve and enjoy.

Nutritional Value (Amount per Serving):

- Calories 170
- Fat 7.6 g
- Carbohydrates 22.5 g
- Sugar 13.1 g
- Protein 7 g
- Cholesterol 10 mg

Peach Raspberry Smoothie

Preparation Time: 5 minutes
Cooking Time: 1 minute
Serve: 1

Ingredients:

- 3/4 cup peach, chopped
- 1 cup raspberries
- 1 tsp honey
- 1/3 cup almond milk
- 1/4 cup Greek yogurt

Directions:

1. Add all ingredients into the blender container. Secure the lid.
2. Start the blending on low speed, then quickly increase to highest speed and blend for 1 minute or until smooth.
3. Serve and enjoy.

Nutritional Value (Amount per Serving):

- Calories 313
- Fat 20 g
- Carbohydrates 35 g
- Sugar 24 g
- Protein 4 g
- Cholesterol 0 mg

Coffee Milkshake

Preparation Time: 5 minutes
Cooking Time: 1 minute
Serve: 2

Ingredients:

- 2 tbsp cocoa powder
- 2 tbsp instant coffee
- 3/4 cup milk
- 4 scoops vanilla ice cream

Directions:

1. Add all ingredients into the blender container. Secure the lid.
2. Start the blending on low speed, then quickly increase to highest speed and blend for 1 minute or until smooth.
3. Serve and enjoy.

Nutritional Value (Amount per Serving):

- Calories 332
- Fat 16 g
- Carbohydrates 39 g
- Sugar 32 g
- Protein 8 g
- Cholesterol 66 mg

Watermelon Strawberry Smoothie

Preparation Time: 5 minutes
Cooking Time: 1 minute
Serve: 2

Ingredients:

- 3 1/2 cups watermelon
- 8 oz strawberries

Directions:

1. Add all ingredients into the blender container. Secure the lid.
2. Start the blending on low speed, then quickly increase to highest speed and blend for 1 minute or until smooth.
3. Serve and enjoy.

Nutritional Value (Amount per Serving):

- Calories 116
- Fat 0.7 g
- Carbohydrates 28.7 g
- Sugar 21 g
- Protein 2.3 g
- Cholesterol 0 mg

Mix Berry Smoothie

Preparation Time: 5 minutes
Cooking Time: 1 minute
Serve: 2

Ingredients:

- 1 banana
- 1/2 cup blueberries
- 1/2 cup raspberries
- 1 cup strawberries
- 1 cup almond milk
- 1/4 tsp vanilla

Directions:

1. Add all ingredients into the blender container. Secure the lid.
2. Start the blending on low speed, then quickly increase to highest speed and blend for 1 minute or until smooth.
3. Serve and enjoy.

Nutritional Value (Amount per Serving):

- Calories 390
- Fat 29.4 g
- Carbohydrates 34.7 g
- Sugar 19.8 g
- Protein 4.5 g
- Cholesterol 0 mg

Healthy Tropical Smoothie

Preparation Time: 5 minutes
Cooking Time: 1 minute
Serve: 2

Ingredients:

- 1/2 cup pineapple
- 1/2 cup mango
- 1/2 banana
- 1 tbsp orange juice
- 1/2 cup coconut milk

Directions:

1. Add all ingredients into the blender container. Secure the lid.
2. Start the blending on low speed, then quickly increase to highest speed and blend for 1 minute or until smooth.
3. Serve and enjoy.

Nutritional Value (Amount per Serving):

- Calories 213
- Fat 14.6 g
- Carbohydrates 22.5 g
- Sugar 16 g
- Protein 2.3 g
- Cholesterol 0 mg

Healthy Berry Smoothie

Preparation Time: 5 minutes
Cooking Time: 1 minute
Serve: 2

Ingredients:

- 1/2 cup blueberries
- 1 cup strawberries
- 1 tbsp honey
- 1 cup almond milk
- 1 tbsp chia seeds
- 1/3 cup oats

Directions:

1. Add all ingredients into the blender container. Secure the lid.
2. Start the blending on low speed, then quickly increase to highest speed and blend for 1 minute or until smooth.
3. Serve and enjoy.

Nutritional Value (Amount per Serving):

- Calories 403
- Fat 29.9 g
- Carbohydrates 35.3 g
- Sugar 19.9 g
- Protein 5.3 g
- Cholesterol 0 mg

Easy Strawberry Protein Shake

Preparation Time: 5 minutes
Cooking Time: 1 minute
Serve: 2

Ingredients:

- 8 strawberries
- 5 drops liquid stevia
- 1 tsp vanilla
- 2 1/2 cups almond milk
- 2 scoops whey protein powder

Directions:

1. Add all ingredients into the blender container. Secure the lid.
2. Start the blending on low speed, then quickly increase to highest speed and blend for 1 minute or until smooth.
3. Serve and enjoy.

Nutritional Value (Amount per Serving):

- Calories 216
- Fat 5 g
- Carbohydrates 17 g
- Sugar 11 g
- Protein 23 g
- Cholesterol 65 mg

Healthy Orange Smoothie

Preparation Time: 5 minutes
Cooking Time: 1 minute
Serve: 1

Ingredients:

- 1 cup orange juice
- 1/2 cup carrots, chopped
- 1/2 tsp turmeric
- 1 tsp ginger, minced
- 1 banana

Directions:

1. Add all ingredients into the blender container. Secure the lid.
2. Start the blending on low speed, then quickly increase to highest speed and blend for 1 minute or until smooth.
3. Serve and enjoy.

Nutritional Value (Amount per Serving):

- Calories 250
- Fat 1.1 g
- Carbohydrates 60.1 g
- Sugar 38 g
- Protein 3.7 g
- Cholesterol 0 mg

Peach Lemonade

Preparation Time: 5 minutes
Cooking Time: 1 minute
Serve: 2

Ingredients:

- 2 cups peach slices
- 1 cup ice cubes
- 2 lemon juice
- 1/4 cup sugar

Directions:

1. Add all ingredients into the blender container. Secure the lid.
2. Start the blending on low speed, then quickly increase to highest speed and blend for 1 minute or until desired consistency.
3. Serve and enjoy.

Nutritional Value (Amount per Serving):

- Calories 153
- Fat 0.4 g
- Carbohydrates 39 g
- Sugar 39 g
- Protein 1.4 g
- Cholesterol 0 mg

Mango Pineapple Peach Smoothie

Preparation Time: 5 minutes
Cooking Time: 1 minute
Serve: 2

Ingredients:

- 1/2 cup mango
- 1/2 cup pineapple
- 1/2 cup peaches
- 2 tbsp protein powder
- 1/2 tbsp honey
- 1 tbsp ginger, grated
- 3/4 cup coconut milk
- 1/2 tbsp lemon zest
- 1 lemon juice

Directions:

1. Add all ingredients into the blender container. Secure the lid.
2. Start the blending on low speed, then quickly increase to highest speed and blend for 1 minute or until smooth.
3. Serve and enjoy.

Nutritional Value (Amount per Serving):

- Calories 293
- Fat 21 g
- Carbohydrates 26 g
- Sugar 20 g
- Protein 3 g
- Cholesterol 0 mg

Cinnamon Apple Smoothie

Preparation Time: 5 minutes
Cooking Time: 1 minute
Serve: 2

Ingredients:

- 2 apples, sliced
- 1 cup ice cubes
- 3/4 tsp ground cinnamon
- 1/2 tsp vanilla
- 1 1/2 tbsp chia seeds
- 2 tbsp almond butter
- 1/3 cup rolled oats
- 1 1/2 cups almond milk

Directions:

1. Add all ingredients into the blender container. Secure the lid.
2. Start the blending on low speed, then quickly increase to highest speed and blend for 1 minute or until smooth.
3. Serve and enjoy.

Nutritional Value (Amount per Serving):

- Calories 685
- Fat 53 g
- Carbohydrates 53 g
- Sugar 30 g
- Protein 9 g
- Cholesterol 0 mg

Banana Peanut Butter Smoothie

Preparation Time: 5 minutes
Cooking Time: 1 minute
Serve: 2

Ingredients:

- 1 1/2 cups almond milk
- 1 cup ice
- 1 tbsp cocoa powder
- 1/2 tsp vanilla
- 2 tbsp Greek yogurt
- 2 tbsp peanut butter
- 2 bananas

Directions:

1. Add all ingredients into the blender container. Secure the lid.
2. Start the blending on low speed, then quickly increase to highest speed and blend for 1 minute or until smooth.
3. Serve and enjoy.

Nutritional Value (Amount per Serving):

- Calories 622
- Fat 51 g
- Carbohydrates 41 g
- Sugar 22 g
- Protein 9 g
- Cholesterol 0 mg

Healthy Avocado Spinach Smoothie

Preparation Time: 5 minutes
Cooking Time: 1 minute
Serve: 2

Ingredients:

- 2 cups spinach
- 3/4 cup almond milk
- 1 tbsp almond butter
- 1/2 avocado, scoop out the flesh
- 1 banana

Directions:

1. Add all ingredients into the blender container. Secure the lid.
2. Start the blending on low speed, then quickly increase to highest speed and blend for 1 minute or until smooth.
3. Serve and enjoy.

Nutritional Value (Amount per Serving):

- Calories 418
- Fat 36.1 g
- Carbohydrates 25.4 g
- Sugar 11 g
- Protein 6.2 g
- Cholesterol 0 mg

Sweet Avocado Smoothie

Preparation Time: 5 minutes
Cooking Time: 1 minute
Serve: 2

Ingredients:

- 2 avocados, scoop out the flesh
- 1 cup ice
- 1 cup almond milk
- 1/3 cup condensed milk

Directions:

1. Add all ingredients into the blender container. Secure the lid.
2. Start the blending on low speed, then quickly increase to highest speed and blend for 1 minute or until smooth.
3. Serve and enjoy.

Nutritional Value (Amount per Serving):

- Calories 500
- Fat 38 g
- Carbohydrates 37 g
- Sugar 31 g
- Protein 7 g
- Cholesterol 17 mg

Healthy Raspberry Smoothie

Preparation Time: 5 minutes
Cooking Time: 1 minute
Serve: 2

Ingredients:

- 2 cups raspberries
- 1 cup yogurt
- 1 cup almond milk
- 1 lime juice
- 1 lime zest
- 1 tbsp honey

Directions:

1. Add all ingredients into the blender container. Secure the lid.
2. Start the blending on low speed, then quickly increase to highest speed and blend for 1 minute or until smooth.
3. Serve and enjoy.

Nutritional Value (Amount per Serving):

- Calories 459
- Fat 30.9 g
- Carbohydrates 38.6 g
- Sugar 26.7 g
- Protein 11.2 g
- Cholesterol 7 mg

Spinach Cucumber Smoothie

Preparation Time: 5 minutes
Cooking Time: 1 minute
Serve: 4

Ingredients:

- 1 avocado, scoop out the flesh
- 1 cucumber
- 1 1/2 cups spinach
- 1 apple, diced
- 4 dates, pitted
- 2 cups almond milk

Directions:

1. Add all ingredients into the blender container. Secure the lid.
2. Start the blending on low speed, then quickly increase to highest speed and blend for 1 minute or until smooth.
3. Serve and enjoy.

Nutritional Value (Amount per Serving):

- Calories 445
- Fat 38 g
- Carbohydrates 28 g
- Sugar 16 g
- Protein 4.9 g
- Cholesterol 0 mg

Healthy Oatmeal Smoothie

Preparation Time: 5 minutes
Cooking Time: 1 minute
Serve: 2

Ingredients:

- 1/4 cup quick oats
- 1/2 tsp cinnamon
- 1/2 tsp vanilla
- 1/4 cup maple syrup
- 1 tbsp peanut butter
- 1/2 cup almond milk
- 1 banana
- Pinch of salt

Directions:

1. Add all ingredients into the blender container. Secure the lid.
2. Start the blending on low speed, then quickly increase to highest speed and blend for 1 minute or until smooth.
3. Serve and enjoy.

Nutritional Value (Amount per Serving):

- Calories 261
- Fat 5 g
- Carbohydrates 51 g
- Sugar 33 g
- Protein 4 g
- Cholesterol 51 mg

Mango Strawberry Smoothie

Preparation Time: 5 minutes
Cooking Time: 1 minute
Serve: 2

Ingredients:

- 1/2 cup strawberry
- 1/2 cup mango
- 1 tbsp honey
- 1 cup orange juice
- 3 tbsp water
- 3/4 cup orange juice

Directions:

1. Add all ingredients into the blender container. Secure the lid.
2. Start the blending on low speed, then quickly increase to highest speed and blend for 1 minute or until smooth.
3. Serve and enjoy.

Nutritional Value (Amount per Serving):

- Calories 166
- Fat 0.7 g
- Carbohydrates 40.2 g
- Sugar 34.2 g
- Protein 2.1 g
- Cholesterol 0 mg

Cookie Shake

Preparation Time: 5 minutes
Cooking Time: 1 minute
Serve: 1

Ingredients:

- 1 chocolate graham cracker, crushed
- 1/2 cup almond milk
- 1 1/2 cups ice cubes
- 1 scoop chocolate protein powder
- Pinch of salt

Directions:

1. Add all ingredients into the blender container. Secure the lid.
2. Start the blending on low speed, then quickly increase to highest speed and blend for 1 minute or until smooth.
3. Serve and enjoy.

Nutritional Value (Amount per Serving):

- Calories 399
- Fat 32 g
- Carbohydrates 18 g
- Sugar 10 g
- Protein 13 g
- Cholesterol 20 mg

Watermelon Strawberry Smoothie

Preparation Time: 5 minutes
Cooking Time: 1 minute
Serve: 2

Ingredients:

- 1 tbsp hemp seeds
- 3/4 cup yogurt
- 1 cup strawberries
- 4 cups watermelon

Directions:

1. Add all ingredients into the blender container. Secure the lid.
2. Start the blending on low speed, then quickly increase to highest speed and blend for 1 minute or until smooth.
3. Serve and enjoy.

Nutritional Value (Amount per Serving):

- Calories 180
- Fat 1.7 g
- Carbohydrates 34.8 g
- Sugar 28.7 g
- Protein 7.5 g
- Cholesterol 6 mg

Cinnamon Banana Smoothie

Preparation Time: 5 minutes
Cooking Time: 1 minute
Serve: 2

Ingredients:

- 1 banana
- 1/2 cup ice
- 1/8 tsp cinnamon
- 1/3 tsp vanilla
- 1/4 cup walnuts
- 1/3 cup rolled oats
- 1 cup almond milk
- 1 apple, peel & dice
- Pinch of salt

Directions:

1. Add all ingredients into the blender container. Secure the lid.
2. Start the blending on low speed, then quickly increase to highest speed and blend for 1 minute or until smooth.
3. Serve and enjoy.

Nutritional Value (Amount per Serving):

- Calories 537
- Fat 39.1 g
- Carbohydrates 46 g
- Sugar 23 g
- Protein 9.3 g
- Cholesterol 0 mg

Thick & Creamy Banana Smoothie

Preparation Time: 5 minutes
Cooking Time: 1 minute
Serve: 2

Ingredients:

- 2 bananas
- 2 tbsp maple syrup
- 1/2 cup almond milk
- 1 cup Greek yogurt

Directions:

1. Add all ingredients into the blender container. Secure the lid.
2. Start the blending on low speed, then quickly increase to highest speed and blend for 1 minute or until smooth.
3. Serve and enjoy.

Nutritional Value (Amount per Serving):

- Calories 295
- Fat 14.7 g
- Carbohydrates 43.7 g
- Sugar 28.3 g
- Protein 2.7 g
- Cholesterol 0 mg

Creamy Cherry Smoothie

Preparation Time: 5 minutes
Cooking Time: 1 minute
Serve: 2

Ingredients:

- 1 1/2 cups cherries
- 1 cup Greek yogurt
- 1 banana
- 1 1/2 cups apple juice

Directions:

1. Add all ingredients into the blender container. Secure the lid.
2. Start the blending on low speed, then quickly increase to highest speed and blend for 1 minute or until smooth.
3. Serve and enjoy.

Nutritional Value (Amount per Serving):

- Calories 163
- Fat 0.6 g
- Carbohydrates 40 g
- Sugar 29 g
- Protein 1.3 g
- Cholesterol 0 mg

Green Pineapple Smoothie

Preparation Time: 5 minutes
Cooking Time: 1 minute
Serve: 2

Ingredients:

- 1/2 cup pineapple
- 1 banana
- 1/2 cup mango
- 2 cups spinach
- 1 cup almond milk
- 1 cup Greek yogurt

Directions:

1. Add all ingredients into the blender container. Secure the lid.
2. Start the blending on low speed, then quickly increase to highest speed and blend for 1 minute or until smooth.
3. Serve and enjoy.

Nutritional Value (Amount per Serving):

- Calories 381
- Fat 29.1 g
- Carbohydrates 32.8 g
- Sugar 21.1 g
- Protein 4.8 g
- Cholesterol 0 mg

Creamy Strawberry Milkshake

Preparation Time: 5 minutes
Cooking Time: 1 minute
Serve: 2

Ingredients:

- 1/2 lb strawberries
- 1/2 cup milk
- 1 tsp vanilla
- 2 cups vanilla ice cream
- 1 1/2 tbsp sugar

Directions:

1. Add all ingredients into the blender container. Secure the lid.
2. Start the blending on low speed, then quickly increase to highest speed and blend for 1 minute or until smooth.
3. Serve and enjoy.

Nutritional Value (Amount per Serving):

- Calories 244
- Fat 8.6 g
- Carbohydrates 37 g
- Sugar 31 g
- Protein 5 g
- Cholesterol 34 mg

Banana Kiwi Smoothie

Preparation Time: 5 minutes
Cooking Time: 1 minute
Serve: 2

Ingredients:

- 1 banana
- 1 cup ice cubes
- 1 cup Greek yogurt
- 1 lime juice
- 1/2 cup almond milk
- 2 kiwi, peel & chopped

Directions:

1. Add all ingredients into the blender container. Secure the lid.
2. Start the blending on low speed, then quickly increase to highest speed and blend for 1 minute or until smooth.
3. Serve and enjoy.

Nutritional Value (Amount per Serving):

- Calories 237
- Fat 14.9 g
- Carbohydrates 27 g
- Sugar 16 g
- Protein 2.9 g
- Cholesterol 0 mg

Easy Pineapple Lemonade

Preparation Time: 5 minutes
Cooking Time: 1 minute
Serve: 2

Ingredients:

- 2 cups pineapple chunks
- 1 cup ice cubes
- 1 lemon juice

Directions:

1. Add all ingredients into the blender container. Secure the lid.
2. Start the blending on low speed, then quickly increase to highest speed and blend for 1 minute or until smooth.
3. Serve and enjoy.

Nutritional Value (Amount per Serving):

- Calories 82
- Fat 0.2 g
- Carbohydrates 21.7 g
- Sugar 16.3 g
- Protein 0.9 g
- Cholesterol 0 mg

www.ingramcontent.com/pod-product-compliance
Lightning Source LLC
Chambersburg PA
CBHW082040080526
44578CB00009B/757